100% ME

A DORLING KINDERSLEY BOOK

LONDON, NEW YORK,
MELBOURNE, MUNICH, and DELHI

Written and edited by Elinor Greenwood and Alexander Cox
Design Claire Patané, Rachael Smith, Clémence de Molliens, Hedi Gutt, Gemma Fletcher,
Sadie Thomas, Emma Forge, Tom Forge, and Clare Harris

Production editor Sean Daly
Jacket designer Jess Bentall
Jacket editor Mariza O'Keeffe
Design manager Rachael Foster
Publishing manager Bridget Giles

Consultant Mary-Jo Hill

First published in Great Britain in 2009 by Dorling Kindersley Limited,
80 Strand, London, WC2R 0RL

2 4 6 8 10 9 7 5 3 1
AD352 – 10/08

A CIP catalogue record for this book is available
from the British Library

ISBN: 978-1-40532-190-7

Colour reproduction by MDP, United Kingdom
Printed and bound by Leo Paper Products Ltd, China

Discover more at
www.dk.com

The publisher would like to thank the following for their kind permission to reproduce their photographs:
(Key: a–above; b–below/bottom; c–centre; f–far; l–left; r–right; t–top)

Alamy Images: Elmtree Images 57cra; Foodfolio 42cr, 94br; D. Hurst 42bl; Mode Images Limited / Richard Gleed 28–
29 (background). **Corbis:** Darama 74cl; Peter M. Fisher 51bl; Lawrence Manning 26 (background), 27 (background), 76
(background), 77 (background); Mika / Zefa 88–89; Redlink 49clb; Emma Rian / Zefa 34r; Gregor Schuster / Zefa 30–31
(background). **DK Images:** Simon Brown 41fbl. **Getty Images:** Photographer's Choice / Jacobs Stock Photography
17crb; Photonica / Gregor Schuster 8–9b, 62–63b; Riser / Tom Fowlks 82–83; Science Faction / William Radcliffe 58c,
59c; Stone / Francesco Reginato 74t (background); Stone / Tim Flach 9tr, 63tr; Stone+ / Matthias Clamer 72–73; Taxi /
Andy Reynolds 84–85; Taxi / Walter Wick 66c. **Carrie Love:** 44l, 45r. **PunchStock:** Corbis 32–33, 52–53; Digital Vision
/ B2M Productions 51br; Digital Vision / Jessica Wedvick 61cb, 94fbl; Pixland 21tc, 36bl; Stockbyte 6–7 (background),
38–39 (background), 60–61 (background). **Science Photo Library:** John Bavosi 55c, 95bl. **Shutterstock:** 3d_kot 86
(buttons); 78br; Aliciahh 86bl, 86br, 86cla, 86clb, 86cra, 86crb; Michael D. Brown 87br, 87tl; Drawperfect 58bl, 58cl, 59cl;
Fee Graphic 96; Christos Georghiou 59br; Viktor Gmyria 87clb; Sabri Deniz Kizil 12cra; Georgijevic Miroslav 48clb;
Monkey Business Images 4bl; NatUlrich 18tr, 19tr; Pepita 57fcla.
All other images © Dorling Kindersley. For further information see: www.dkimages.com

100% girl 6 – 37

100% me 38 – 59

100% boy 60 – 91

Foreword

100% Me is a book for everyone who is coming up to or in the first stages of puberty. This time of your life can be a minefield of problems that range from feeling tearful to falling out with friends, and worrying about all the changes your body is going through. Whatever you feel now, you can be pretty sure someone else has felt it too, and in this book you get all the reassurance and information you need to take puberty in your stride.

From your love life to your life cycle, there is stuff in here that you really need to know about, as well as lots of fun quizzes and cool graphics. Because the book has three sections, one for the girls, one for the boys, and one for both sexes, the girls can find out about the boys, and vice versa. So, flip through the pages, find out what you want to know, and remember that *100% Me* is **100% for YOU**.

How to use this book

Girls and boys are different, that's a fact, and they go through puberty in a different way. For this reason this book is divided into three sections: one for the girls, one for both sexes, and one for the boys.

In the girls section, you can find out about breasts and periods, sex hormones, and biology, as well as explore the feelings and issues that commonly concern girls.

In the section for both sexes, you can find out about the facts of life and issues that range from anorexia to acne. Everything in this section applies to both sexes

In the boys section, you can find out about your voice breaking, erections, shaving, sex hormones, and biology, as well as explore the feelings and issues that commonly concern boys.

100% Girl

MY new bra is so uncomfortable!

P20

Shall I try and get out of gym today?

P32

can't stop thinking about him.

P28

P24

Uh-oh, I think I just got MY period.

P12

Why do I feel so moody?

What makes *girls* girls?

It's plain to see that girls are different to boys. So what makes girls girls? Girls' and boys' bodies are generally made up of the same stuff, but with four important differences.

① hormones

Oestrogen (pronounced "east-row-jin") is the female sex hormone that causes most of the changes during puberty. Progesterone, oestrogen, and other hormones work together to control the menstrual cycle.

② sex organs

A girl's sex organs are inside her body, unlike a boy's. The brain makes female sex hormones and the ovaries produce eggs. Tubes join the ovaries to the womb. The vagina is a canal leading to the womb. Women also have breasts that are capable of feeding a baby with milk.

The ovaries release an egg every month. If the egg is fertilized by a man's sperm, it will develop into a baby inside the womb. If it is unfertilized, it leaves the body during menstruation (see pages 24–25).

fallopian tube · egg · ovary · womb · ovary · vagina

③ the brain

Scientists have long been interested in testing for differences between the brains of girls and boys.

There are physical differences between girls' and boys' brains. Girls' brains are smaller (though this is proved to have no effect on intelligence – sorry boys!). During puberty girls' brains also mature earlier than boys' brains do (though the boys catch up relatively quickly).

④ chromosomes

The sex chromosomes are one of the 23 pairs you have inside every body cell. Sex chromosomes are shaped like the letters X or Y. They determine whether you are a girl or a boy. You inherit one chromosome from each parent. If you have two Xs, then you're a girl. If you had an X and a Y, then you would be a boy.

X Chromosomes

You have a pair of XX chromosomes in every body cell. That means every body cell – and there are over 10 trillion of them altogether – "knows" you are a girl!

Body talk

Our bodies change all the time throughout our lives. Women have four stages in their life cycle.

Our genes, stringed together in strands of DNA inside every body cell, have a say in when we reach puberty or the menopause.

2 Puberty

Puberty is when your body matures into an adult and you start your periods. It's a transition phase that leaves your body capable of having a baby.

1 Childhood

The first stage is childhood, from when you were born until the start of puberty.

Body shapes

Our bodies are all sorts of shapes and sizes. Yours is destined to be a certain body type – it's in your genes! Which one do you think is most like you?

The Hourglass
Curvy hips and bust and a narrow waist.

The Pear
Narrow shoulders, wide hips, thighs, and bottom.

3
Maturity
When you are an adult and are fully grown.

4
Menopause
The menopause happens when a woman's periods stop, and she can no longer have a baby.

GIRL POWER

Body put-down free zone

However you turn out, try not to be negative about your body. Who you are is FAR more important than what you look like. *Consider these points:*

>> Take average height–weight ratios with a pinch of salt. Your correct weight is the one you're comfortable with and that allows you to live a happy, healthy, and active life.

>> We are bombarded with touched-up images of styled-up slim women in magazines, adverts, everywhere! These can make us feel that they are normal, and we are not.

>> People can feel bad if they weigh above average, or even average. Or they may feel too thin. There aren't many winners in the game of comparison.

The Apple
Top heavy with a larger bust and tummy but thin legs.

The Tube Shape
Slender, fewer curves, like a typical model!

It all STARTS in your brain.

THE HORMONE

What kick-starts puberty?

1 A gene starts the ball rolling.

The *pituitary gland* and the *ovaries* are hormone factories. They increase production during puberty and that not only changes your body, but can affect your mood too.

2 It wakes up the HORMONES responsible for all the changes experienced during puberty.

DID YOU KNOW?
Hormones are chemical messengers. They tell the cells in your body what to do when.

DID YOU KNOW
Hormones can make you moody and tearful, and fill yo with romantic feelings.

3 There is no going back now!

DID YOU KNOW?
30 different hormones work in your body, regulating such things as your sleep, temperature, and hunger.

4 Let's meet the hormones...

5 GnRH hormone is made in the pituitary gland at the base of your brain. This hormone works constantly throughout puberty.

6 Human growth hormone, also made in the pituitary gland, does just what its name suggests – it makes you grow!

7 Oestrogen is the female sex hormone. It is made in the ovaries and causes most of the changes to your body durin puberty.

FACTORY

ollow the numbers round to find out.

16
average age 15½
adult breast size
usual age 12-19

15
average age 13
first period
usual age 10-16

WELCOME TO THE HORMONE FACTORY!

The pituitary gland sends hormones to the ovaries that make them come to life. Then the ovaries send hormones to the rest of the body, telling it to start changing.

brain

pituitary gland

ovaries

14
average age 13
underarm hair appears
usual age 10-16

13
average age 12½
hips widen, body gets curvier
usual age 8-15

12
average age 12¼
growth spurt **peaks**
usual age 8-14

Progesterone is also made in the ovaries and works with oestrogen. Its job is to help control the menstrual cycle (periods).

9
Here's how your body changes...

10
average age 11¼
breasts start to grow
usual age 8-14

11
average age 11¾
pubic hair starts to appear
usual age 9-15

GIRL >> WOMAN

START HERE

Puberty can start anytime between the ages of 7 and 13. 10½ is the average age.

One sign that things are about to happen is that you start to grow taller more quickly.

The skin around your nipples gets bigger and darker.

Your skin is oily and sweaty. You'll need to use deodorant.

Oh no! SPOTS!!! You may get more zits...

Romantic feelings!

Breasts grow some more. Take a look at them from the side.

Hormones surging!

Periods may bring PMT (pre-menstrual tension) and period pain, and make you feel rotten.

...especially before your period.

You are getting curvy now as your body fat moves to your hips, buttocks, and thighs.

Not all girls have hourglass figures – it depends on your genes. Some girls have big breasts, some have small, and some have medium!

Puberty can be a *challenge*, so it's good to know what to expect, when. Follow the *arrows* to learn the *stages*. (Keep in mind that this is a general guide. Everybody is different.)

Your nipples become raised and your breasts start to grow.

A few long, downy hairs appear between your legs. These are your first pubic hairs.

A sprinkling of underarm hair appears too (though this can come anytime – and over a period of months and years, rather than overnight).

NEXT...

Peak height growth time – you are shooting up!

Your periods could start anytime now.

Maybe by 10 cm (4 in) in a year, or more!

Your breasts start to fill out.

You may find you become a bit fatter. This is normal and will disappear in the next stage...

Feel emotional? Get upset easily? Hormones might be to blame.

WELL DONE... *you made it!*

Now you can enjoy some of the good things about getting older.

Vrrroom!

15

Growing UP

Puberty means you are *growing into an adult* and your body is changing into a woman's. But how is it growing? Which specific bits? And what will your body be like when it's finished?

Boob facts

• It takes on average two to three years for your breasts to bud.
• If you start puberty early, your breast growth may slow down and even stop for a few years while they are still buds.
• When you gently squeeze your breasts between your thumb and index finger, if there is over 1 cm (0.5 in) of tissue, it is likely that your breasts are starting to grow and puberty has begun.

Am I normal?

You may feel you are not growing quickly enough, or too quickly. You look in the mirror and think: "Am I normal?" The answer to that is no one is normal! Look around you – everyone is completely different.

Getting boobs

The first stage of puberty is an exciting one – your breasts start to grow! There are five stages of breast development (on a measure called the Tanner scale).

Stage 1
Before puberty – there is no breast tissue.

Stage 2
"Breast bud" stage – there is a small mound of breast tissue under the nipple, and the part around the nipple, called the areola, is starting to grow bigger.

Stage 3
The breast and areola grow bigger still – the nipple does not yet stick out.

Stage 4
The areola and nipple begin to stick out from the breast. (Some girls skip this stage.)

Stage 5
Breasts are fully grown. Now only the nipple sticks out. The areola is back level with the rest of the breast.

Getting hairier

Pubic hair (and underarm hair) can start growing even if puberty hasn't started yet. This is because their growth is not ruled by the puberty hormone, oestrogen, but by a quite different hormone. Here are the Tanner stages.

Stage 1

No pubic hair.

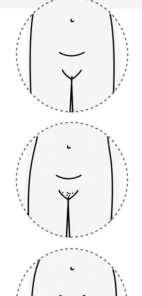

Stage 2

Sparse growth along the sides of the opening of the vagina. These dark hairs can be straight or slightly curled.

Stage 3

Hair is darker and curlier and now spreads thinly over the pubic area.

Stage 4

Hair is thicker and looks like an adult's, but covers a much smaller area.

Stage 5

Hair is adult in quantity and type, and looks like an upside-down triangle.

Getting taller

Before puberty begins, you have been growing by about 5 cm (2 in) a year, but once it gets going, you shoot up – by about 10 cm (4 in) a year! In many girls, this happens sometime between ages 10 and 12, but it really varies. You may shoot past the boys, only to be overtaken two to three years later, when the boys have their growth spurt.

There's a good chance your body will look similar to either your mum's or dad's.

It's in your genes

We can't choose how we look – it was decided for us when we were created. Your parents passed on their genes and those genes helped to decide your size and shape, your eye colour, even whether you have freckles or not. Your height is just one of your features decided by your genes.

The *boob* basics

You and your breasts are together for life. And puberty is when they make their appearance. *Big or small*, eagerly anticipated, or somewhat dreaded, breasts are two bumps on a person's body that *can seem like a very big deal.*

When do they start to grow?

Breasts can start growing at any age between 8 and 13, and everyone grows them at different rates. This can be tough if you are 11, your best friend is fully developed, and you're still flat chested. Rest assured that nature will take its course and you will get your adult breasts eventually.

What are they for?

Your breasts are part of your reproductive system. They mean that someday if you have a baby your breasts will make milk that your baby needs to survive.

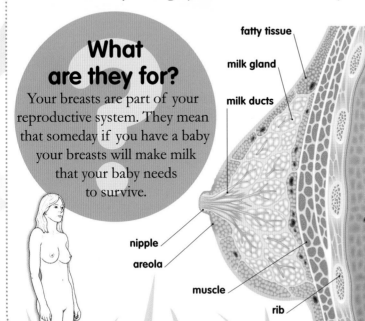

- fatty tissue
- milk gland
- milk ducts
- nipple
- areola
- muscle
- rib

A girl's *breast friends*

You may love your new breasts, or you may barely notice them. But some women find fault with their breasts. Girls with big breasts may feel uncomfortable lying on their front, or jiggling as they run, while girls with smaller chests may feel less womanly. But, big or small, your breasts are part of you and the best way forward is to learn to love them.

Growing pains

Issue	Advice
One is growing faster than the other	Don't worry about this as they usually even out later. Even if you end up with one breast bigger than the other, this is normal and probably only you will notice.
Your breasts feel sore and tender	This is perfectly normal and due to hormones. It can be especially noticeable before and during your period.
Your breasts feel lumpy	This is usually normal, but don't hesitate to talk to a doctor or school nurse, if you are worried.
Unusually large breasts	If you feel your breasts are particularly large, you'll probably just grow into them. Occasionally though, this can be caused by a rare condition called "pubertal macromastia". Get checked out by a doctor if you are concerned.
Stretch marks	As your breasts grow you may see fine lines appearing on them. These will fade away with time.
Nipples that don't stick out	Teenagers often have flat nipples that will stick out later. An "inverted nipple" is when the nipple is tucked in to the breast. Boys can have these too. This is just the way you are and lots of other women are the same (about 10%).
Hairy nipples	Long dark hairs around the nipple are quite common in men and women. You can pluck or cut them if they bother you.

BRA shopping

Shopping for a bra can be *bewildering*. There are *many types* to choose from, and the *sizing isn't that straightforward*. It has been estimated that about 75–80% of women do not wear a properly fitting bra. So follow this guide to choosing a comfortable and correctly fitting bra – *it's an important skill for life*.

<< First bras

You may want to buy a bra when your chest starts to develop, or if you haven't started to develop but would like to wear a bra. First bras have flat or nearly flat cups and can be found in their own section in bra shops or department stores.

<< Soft-cup bras

These don't usually have underwires and are comfortable, but may not completely control any bounce or jiggling. They come in lots of different fabrics and thicknesses.

<< Underwire bras

These are not recommended as a first bra and need to be carefully fitted so the wires (which are sewn in along the lower edge and sides) don't dig in. However, a comfortable underwire bra lifts and holds breasts well and looks smooth under tops.

<< Sports bras

These are often a good first-bra option too. They don't have traditional cups and are very comfy. Good sports bras give excellent support and are often designed to keep you cool. For larger breasts, sports bras with moulded cups work best.

fit tips

Breasts should not spill out of the sides or top. If they do, the cups are too small.

The cups should not wrinkle or pucker. If they do, the cups are too big.

The middle of the bra should sit on your chest.

The straps adjust to allow you to change the fit for each breast.

You should be able to slip two fingers under the band at the back. The band should be in the middle of your back (not pulling high or slipping low).

Many bra shops offer a free fitting service which is really worth taking up. It's also good to know how to measure yourself. Here's how.

Measuring the BAND size >

You need a tape measure. *Wrap it* around your *ribcage* right *under your breasts*. Be sure the tape is even and not hiked up at the back. The tape should be snug, not tight. Take the measurement in inches rather than centimetres as bra sizes are always given in inches.

< Measuring the CUP size

Measure around your breasts at the *fullest part* (probably at the nipple level). If the band size is larger than the measurement around your nipples, your cup size is AAA. If the band size and the measurement around your nipples are the same, your cup size is AA.

If the band size is smaller than the cup measurement, *use this guide.* >

up to 2.5 cm (1 in) = A
up to 5 cm (2 in) = B
up to 8 cm (3 in) = C
up to 10 cm (4 in) = D
up to 13 cm (5 in) = DD
up to 15 cm (6 in) = E

Inside and out

Unlike a man's, a woman's sex organs are hard to see. So let's take a look and find out what they are all about.

on the outside...

This is your own body and it is natural to want to see what it looks like. So take a look! The best way to see between your legs, is to grab a mirror, and follow this guide to your vulva.

female **SEX** *organs*

CLITORIS
This is a small mound of skin the size of a pea. It is the most sensitive to touching and sexual feelings.

URETHRA
A small opening through which urine (wee) from the bladder leaves the body.

LABIA
These are the flaps of skin that cover the openings to the vagina, urethra, and clitoris.

VAGINAL OPENING
This is the opening of the passageway from the female sex organs to the outside of the body. It is bigger than the opening to the urethra.

THE HYMEN
At the entrance to your vagina, you may see a thin membrane of skin with one or more openings. This is called a hymen. This is often broken during a girl's first experience of sexual intercourse. But it can be torn or stretched after an accident, or by exercise like gymnastics or horse riding without a girl even noticing.

on the inside...

A woman's sex organs lie inside her pelvis and are made up of two ovaries which connect to her womb (uterus), and vagina. The different parts all do different jobs.

fallopian tube egg fallopian tube

site of
egg release

ovary

uterus

uterine lining

cervix

vagina

ovary

OVARIES
Your ovaries are where eggs are made. All the eggs you will ever have are stored in your ovaries when you are born. They mature at puberty, and are then released one by one.

UTERUS
This hollow pear-sized muscle is where babies can grow. It is sometimes called the womb.

VAGINA
This is the passage from the uterus to the outside of a woman's body.

CERVIX
The cervix is a small opening at the lower end of the uterus. It connects the uterus to the vagina, and can open wide when a baby is born.

FALLOPIAN TUBES
Each tube is about 7.5 cm (3 in) long, and the width of a drinking straw. They connect the ovaries to the uterus.

What's a na na?
The female genitals have always been an awkward subject. Some people feel embarrassed to say vagina and slang words are the result. Here are some common (and not-so-common) ones, just so you know...

kitty
punani
vajayjay
cooter
cha cha
coochie
muff
hoo ha
down there
front bottom
box
bits and pieces
lady business
goodies
na na
lala
cho cho
fanny

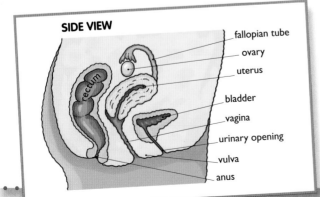

SIDE VIEW
fallopian tube
ovary
uterus
rectum
bladder
vagina
urinary opening
vulva
anus

MASTURBATION
This is feeling or rubbing genitals in a way that feels good. It may lead to muscles contracting inside the pelvis and an overall feeling of pleasure spreading throughout the body called orgasm. Masturbation can't harm you and is a perfectly normal thing to do.

The female cycle

In nature there are many cycles: that of the moon, the seasons, the water cycle, and the menstrual cycle! That last one applies to us girls. Has yours started? Hasn't it started? From your mum to your mates, everyone suddenly wants to know.

The science bit

As a woman releases an egg each month, the lining of her womb becomes thicker to prepare itself for pregnancy. If the egg is fertilized by a man's sperm, this lining will then gently cushion the egg as it develops into a baby. If the egg is not fertilized, both the egg and lining leave the woman's body through the vagina – and this is what causes the bleeding you experience during your period.

What it means to you

This is the most dramatic step from girl to woman of the whole puberty process. It can make you feel excited, shocked, relieved (at last!), panicked, or a bit of all that. The first thing most girls see in their pants is NOT a great flow of redness. In fact, it is often just brownish red and very light to start with, giving you plenty of time to sort out clothing protection.

Days 6–12

- Oestrogen levels begin to peak.
- The egg continues to mature in the ovary.
- The uterine lining starts to thicken.

egg

tube

ovary

Days 1–5

Menstruation
- Your period begins, usually lasting between 3–6 days.
- On the first day of your period, a new egg begins to mature in one ovary.
- The sac around the maturing egg produces oestrogen, increasing the levels in your body.

Day 22–day 1

egg

- Hormone levels are at their lowest now.
- The inner lining of the uterus starts to fall away, along with the unfertilized egg.

The Menstrual Cycle

6
5
4
3
2
1
28
27
26
25
24
23

Period pain

There is hardly a woman on Earth who hasn't experienced period pain. The pain is caused by the womb contracting, shedding its lining (as a period) so a new lining can grow. There are ways to treat it. Exercise can ease the pain (though you might not feel like it), a hot-water bottle on your lower stomach may do the trick, and, if all else fails, taking painkillers (following the packet instructions) should sort you out. Severe pain should always be reported to a doctor.

Days 13–14　**egg**

Ovulation
• Around day 14 the sac containing the mature egg splits open releasing it from the ovary.
• The empty sac left in the ovary begins to produce both oestrogen and progesterone.
• The uterine lining continues to thicken.

Fertile Time

9 10 11 12 13 14 15 16 17 18 19 20

egg
Day 15–22

• Hormone levels begin to drop again.
• Blood vessels in the uterine wall contract and spasm due to the lack of oestrogen and progesterone. These are period pains.

PMT

PMT is short for pre-menstrual tension and is felt to some degree by three out of four women. It is caused by a hormone imbalance up to two weeks before your period and is not serious. However, it can give you food cravings, headaches, spots, and sore breasts, and make you feel emotional and irritable. A healthy, balanced diet and regular exercise can help. So can diet changes. Ask your doctor if you suffer badly.

Things to know
• There can be much longer gaps between periods when you first start menstruating, and they can be irregular.
• Women have different-length cycles. If your periods are regular, count the days between day 1 of your period, and day 1 of your next period to give you the length of yours.
• Though it may look like a lot, the average amount of blood is only about 2 tablespoons for an entire period.
• About 6 months or so before getting your first period, you might notice odourless, clear or white vaginal discharge.

In the BATHROOM

You may find you are spending more time in the bathroom
– there is *so much more to do there*, what with spots, periods,
and hairy legs! Your siblings may be bashing on the door, but tell
them to wait – what you are doing is important.

MAKE UP

When it comes to make-up, less is more!
A lick of lip gloss, a sweep of blusher, and
a wave of mascara should be enough to
enhance your natural, fresh-faced
beauty. For special occasions,
you could add a bit of glitter
into the mix. Varnishing
your toenails is a fun
place to experiment
with colour.

Top tips
Experiment with
what suits your
skin colour. And
remember to remove
all your make-up
before bedtime!

HAIR REMOVAL

We can't always visit a beautician, and most of us
buy our hair-removal products from the chemist.
These vary a lot. Depilatory (hair-removing) creams
provide a pain-free option, but the results can be
patchy and the creams smelly! Soap applied thickly
to damp legs and armpits, then shaved with a razor
is a fuss-free answer. Self-waxing can be painful (but
the effects last longer – up to 4 weeks).

SHAVING
Always use a sharp
razor, as a blunt one
is not effective and
can damage your
skin. Don't share
razors and always
be extremely
careful with
them. Nicks
can happen!

WAX
Always closely follow
the manufacturer's
instructions when using
self-waxing kits.

PERIOD PRODUCTS

It's a good idea to keep some sanitary towels handy in case you start your period. (If it starts at school, and you don't have one, ask to visit the school nurse, who will be able to help you.) Girls generally begin by using sanitary towels to catch menstrual blood. These can easily be secured to your pants. When using tampons, wash your hands before and after their use and always read the manufacturer's instructions carefully before using any type of tampon.

When is the right time to start using tampons? Some people have specific ideas regarding this issue, but the general rule is – when you feel you want to.

sanitary towels

These are an easy-to-use answer to catching blood and work like a wad of absorbent cotton wool. You may think they are big and bulky and that everyone must surely be noticing your bulging crotch, but that is not the case. No one will notice them.

tampons

Choose the slimmest available tampons when you are starting to use them and wait until the heavy part of your period before inserting one. Try and relax. If you are tense it makes putting a tampon in more difficult.

PERSONAL HYGIENE

After the start of puberty, you sweat more, and your skin produces more oil from oil glands. This can start to smell and produce body odour (B.O.). This is easily avoided by washing every day, especially after sport and by using a good deodorant.

a white smile

Now you have your adult teeth, you need to look after them. Clean your teeth twice a day and get into the habit of flossing between them. This helps you avoid tooth decay and bad breath.

sweet smelling

Deodorant allows you to sweat but prevents odours. Anti-perspirant stops your sweat glands from sweating.

feet

Also, remember to keep your feet clean and always wear socks in trainers.

body sprays

Body sprays help to mask any bad smells. They are a bit like cheap perfumes. Remember not to spray too much!

LOVE life

Puberty marks the start of you as a woman — and the beginning of your *love life*. You may begin to have strong romantic feelings early in adolescence, or you may experience none at all. **Both are normal**. One thing to bear in mind is that you are just at the beginning of your love life, and this will last for the rest of your life, so there is really *no hurry!*

Crushes

A crush is an intense, joyous feeling you get when you think about someone. You may get a crush on someone for a short time only, or a crush can be intense and long lasting. If you have a crush, you may dream about a relationship together and obsess over your crush. It can be magical, painful, and torturous. It's like a romantic hero-worship.

Type 1

Many young girls develop crushes on pop stars, or movie stars, teachers, adults, friends' older brothers — the object of the crush is often out of reach. Crushes are a good way to rehearse romantic feelings, without having to approach real-life problems such as how to act or what to say…. Deep down, you know there is unlikely ever to be a relationship.

Type 2

If you develop a crush on someone your own age, who you know, complications can creep in. Should you let him know? Does he like you back? If he does, this can be really exciting – or it can have the opposite effect and put you off him! If you do decide to let him know, test the water first to see if he seems to like you too. Just striking up a casual conversation with him is usually best… and make sure you do it in private. If his mates are there listening, he may act cool.

Don't be crushed by a crush!

You may experience the misery of having your feelings rejected. This is never a happy situation, and can make you even more besotted than you were before. Here are a few tips to make sure your life doesn't fall apart:

1. **Confide** in your **friends** and ask them to distract you.
2. Throw yourself into your schoolwork and make sure you don't fall behind.
3. Take up a new *hobby* – something that gets you out of the house and gets you moving.
4. Give yourself allotted time alone to fantasize about your crush, but *don't let it take over your life.*

Just good friends

After you reach a certain age, and you are friends with a boy, it may attract unwanted attention – even if you have known him all your life! Even adults may gently tease you, and ask "Is he your boyfriend?". You can ignore this, or explain you really are just good friends, there is nothing else to it!

Gay and straight

Sometimes girls develop crushes on other girls. This is normal too. To add to the confusing emotional rollercoaster that puberty can be, there is not one way to be! From puberty, and especially through the teen years, people need to discover their sexuality.

Heterosexual (straight) means being sexually attracted to the opposite sex. The majority of people are heterosexual.
Homosexual (gay or lesbian) means being sexually attracted to the same sex. One in ten adults is estimated to be homosexual.
Bisexual means being sexually attracted to both sexes.

Having romantic feelings for other girls may make you feel confused, especially if you have heard insulting slang about it. Research has shown that nearly everyone at some point feels romantic about someone of the same sex. Finding out what your natural sexuality is can take time, or you may know for sure straight away. Everyone is different. Being homosexual is not a choice. It is a part of who you are, the same as being heterosexual. Being homosexual is a perfectly healthy, normal, and acceptable way to be.

Karen loves Sam

Are you going to the park after school? xx

29

Is it *True Love?*

or just a crush

Q.1

How many times a day do you think about him?

A. Who? I like more than one person!

B. At least five times.

C. Pretty much every other second.

Q.2

You see him in the playground talking to another girl. How do you react?

A. I don't think anything of it.

B. Fine – it's really cool that he has friends who are girls.

C. Furious! Do those girls really think he's available.

Q.3

How long have you known him?

A. We haven't spoken to each other at all yet.

B. We have known each other for some time.

C. I don't know how we could talk! I am completely tongue-tied whenever he's near!

Mostly As: You are completely crushed out. You are crazy about him, but he may not know you (or he may be your best friend – even more awkward!). Watch out it doesn't take over your life and get some advice if you feel like you could do with some!

Mostly Bs: You are one smitten kitten. You feel confident in your feelings, and how he feels about you. You're cool that you both have your own lives. When you're together, you are yourself with him. This could be love!

Your stomach flips over when you think about him, you can't stop scribbling his name in your diary, and you find it hard to concentrate. What's going on? Is this love, or just a crush...

Q.4

Does he feel the same about you?

A.
I don't know. Maybe, maybe not. I'm not bothered.

B.
Yes. He's told me he does.

C.
No. I don't think he knows of my existence.

Q.5

Your friends are always totally honest with you. What do they have to say about your guy?

A.
They all fancy him too. It's a laugh!

B.
They like him and think we are well suited.

C.
They wish I would stop talking about him and get back to the normal fun me.

Q.6

Have you ever questioned your feelings about him?

A.
I haven't got that far!

B.
Yes, I recognize all his faults and they have no effect on how I feel.

C.
Of course not! There is no need to question my undying love.

Mostly As You are playing it cool. You are having a laugh, and haven't got a serious crush – yet! One might develop, or any interest may peter out, as someone, or something else takes your fancy.

What's the difference? Here it is in a nutshell – a crush is usually baseless and is for superficial reasons, like you think the guy is cute, or you think he's funny. True Love is mutual – you truly know each other and spend time with that person. It feels perfect like it was meant to be!

Keeping FIT

Exercise is an *important part of life*, almost as important as eating, drinking, and sleeping. And during puberty, your body is growing, your muscles are developing, and the strength you get now will stand you in good stead for the rest of your life.

Martial arts

Athletics

Try a new sport

Puberty is when sports you enjoy may fall out of favour (ballet with big breasts may not seem so fun). Now is a good time to try new sports. Karate and martial arts, as well as self-defence classes, make good choices for young girls. So if you're terrible at tennis, and hate hockey, try and find a sport you do like. You can guarantee there is one.

Yoga

Warming up

As you grow older, warming up before exercise becomes more and more important. A child is naturally bendy and stretchy, but, you've probably noticed, adults aren't! Although you're not elderly yet, your bones are growing heavier and longer, so your muscles have more work to do, making them more prone to injury. So warm up first!

Here are some more good reasons to exercise

✳ Your heart and lungs experience a growth spurt, so you can handle more exercise.

✳ Exercise helps you achieve your best weight and counters obesity.

✳ It strengthens your heart, increases your energy levels, and sends more oxygen to all parts of your body.

✳ It helps deposit calcium in your bones – especially important in your teens. This is when you are building up the bone mass that will be with you for life.

✳ Exercise helps with hormonal mood swings, and helps period pain too!

✳ Getting into good exercising habits now can last for life, with immense benefits to your health as you age.

DON'T OVERDO IT!

Exercising too much can become a COMPULSION and links strongly with eating disorders such as ANOREXIA (see pages 44–45).

Puberty can seem like it's all about *perspiration* and **PIMPLES.**

" *It's* pants! "

You feel tired and emotional, and how come one day you're popular, and the next you're not?

Periods can be inconvenient, to say the least. PMT, stomach cramps, let alone bloodstained pants and sheets, you name it…

How you look has taken on a new importance – what happened to just liking you for who you are?

Spots, braces, glasses…

You may feel you're not developing quickly enough… or that you're developing too quickly.

Boys! (You love them really!)

Here are some reasons why it's *pants*, and some reasons why it's not all *that* BAD.

100% girl

"It's great!"

There are chances to make new friends, try out new things, and generally have lots of fun…

It's exciting getting curvy.

You can experiment with make-up and clothes – and express yourself more in the way you look.

More and more independence. Staying out later at night! Having your own money!

And at the end of it all you can start to drive a car, vote and get your voice heard. Puberty is really gradual, it doesn't happen overnight. There's plenty of time to get used to it, and develop.

Dates and parties to go to. You can watch 12-rated films.

Exploding the

Will exercises make my boobs bigger?

No, you can't add inches to your breasts by exercising as breasts are largely fat and milk glands and there's no exercise to grow those. But exercise can make your breasts sit higher on your chest because it builds up the muscles directly below the breasts.

If I sleep on my stomach will my breasts grow more slowly?

No. The eventual size and shape of your breasts is in your genes, as is the rate that they grow at – sleeping on your front cannot slow down their growth.

I'll grow breasts that are the same size as my mum's.

This is not necessarily the case. You could inherit the breasts of your father's mother, or your aunt. Also, a woman's breast size can change when she has children, or loses or puts on weight. Women need to be re-measured for a new bra throughout the different stages of their lives.

MYTHS

Can a tampon pop out?

A tampon cannot disappear into your body. Nor can it fall out. Your vaginal wall is a strong muscle and it holds the tampon in place as it expands inside you.

Does having your period mean you can't do physical activity?

No. While you have your period, you can do any activity. You need to wear a tampon for swimming however.

Boys won't like me if I'm not gorgeous.

When it comes to attracting the opposite sex, it's more important to have healthy self-esteem than big boobs. No one is ever going to look like Barbie or the air-brushed models in fashion mags, so learn to love who you are. Boys may all seem to fancy one or two girls in your class, but that may be because they're superficially glamorous, and admiring them helps the boys to feel as if they fit in. If you're interesting and friendly, and you care about other people, you'll attract friends of both sexes.

Can breasts pop?

No. Breasts cannot pop because they are made of fat and glands.

100% Me

The facts of life

Puberty changes our bodies from child to adult, that much we know. But **WHY** do we need puberty? Why can't we just grow taller to become adults? The answer to this is simple – *babies!* Before puberty we can't have babies, afterwards we can.

The sperm and the egg

A girl can become pregnant after her first period. A period means she is producing eggs. A boy can make a girl pregnant from his first ejaculation. This means he is producing sperm. If an egg and a sperm join together, then a baby can start growing.

HOW DO THEY JOIN TOGETHER?

1. Halfway through a woman's monthly menstrual cycle (see pages 24–25), an egg cell is released from one of her ovaries. It moves slowly along the fallopian tube, towards the uterus.

2. During sexual intercourse a man's erect penis moves up and down inside the vagina until ejaculation happens. About two teaspoonfuls of semen, containing millions of tiny sperm cells, are left in the top of the vagina.

3. Sperm cells swim through the cervix, through the uterus, and along the fallopian tube. Only a few hundred make it to the egg.

4. If one sperm gets into the egg, they join together and fertilization has happened. A baby can now start to grow inside the woman's body.

A baby starts to grow

The fertilized egg starts to divide and grow into a ball of cells, which moves down to the uterus (or womb). The ball of cells settles into the thick lining of the uterus and begins to grow into a baby. This is the start of pregnancy.

Happy birthday!

A baby takes nine months to grow. When it is ready, the uterus contracts in spasms and the baby's head pushes against the woman's cervix until it opens up (this is called labour). Then the baby travels down the vagina and out into the world.

FOOD for thought

Eating healthily is always important, but as you **_grow really fast_** during adolescence, it is even more important! You may find you eat out more away from your parents. Making a conscious effort to adopt **_healthy eating habits_** now will last you for life.

A healthy, balanced diet
Here is a guide to getting the right proportions of food types in your diet. If every meal is balanced out like this, you are doing well.

TIPS
- Eat fruit or vegetables for a snack
- Use low-fat dairy products
- Watch your sugar intake
- Eat more oily fish
- Increase fibre in your diet
- Decrease the use of salt

33% Carbohydrates

33% Fruit & vegetables

12% Meat, fish, & protein

8% Fats & sugar

14% Milk & dairy

What kind of eater are you?

It's breakfast time. Do you...

A. Miss it out, and spend extra time in bed.
B. Stuff a piece of toast in your mouth as you rush out the door.
C. Eat cereal and toast, or eggs and fruit or a smoothie – you know, a proper breakfast!

Sunday lunch. Do you...

A. Take six roast potatoes and slosh on gallons of gravy. No veg thanks!
B. You'll have a bit of everything and gobble it all down.
C. A few potatoes for you, lots of veg (your favourite bit!). A splash of gravy.

You feel the need for a snack. What do you choose?

A. A bar of chocolate.
B. Bread, crisps, whatever is in the cupboard.
C. A piece of fruit, some seeds or nuts.

You are eating out at a diner with friends. What do you choose?

A. Burger and chips.
B. Whatever everyone else is having.
C. Chicken or fish with potatoes and veg.

You're thirsty. What do you drink?

A. A can of sugary fizzy drink.
B. Squash or juice, whatever you can find.
C. A glass of water, or a small glass of fruit juice to add to your 5-a-day.

Mostly Cs

You're a very healthy eater. The habits you have now will last you a lifetime – brilliant!

Mostly Bs

You're a convenience eater. Whatever is available, you'll eat and you don't think much about it, so long as you're full! Try eating more fruit and veg, and be conscious of your 5-a-day.

Mostly As

You're not a very healthy eater. Try to choose more green veg, fruit, lean meats and fish. You'll feel better and learning good habits now can last a lifetime.

Overweight?

Twice as common in adolescents as it was 30 years ago, being very overweight (called obesity) is likely to lead to high blood pressure and type 2 diabetes. Most obese adolescents simply eat too much and exercise too little. Because of society's negative attitudes, many obese adolescents have a poor self-image, and therefore might become less and less active, and then feel more and more alone.

To avoid being overweight try to:
• develop healthy eating habits
• exercise regularly
• not focus on losing a specific amount of weight

Counselling can help adolescents cope with their problems, including poor self-esteem. For help and advice contact your doctor.

the BODY

Too fat? Too thin? Too short? Too tall? Don't worry, your body is going through huge changes, which can be both exciting and frightening.

a cascade of changes

Change is scary and with all the hormones flowing through your body you might start criticising the way you look. You might even start comparing your body to celebrities you see in magazines and on TV. But do they have the perfect body or the body impossible?

thin or false?

Celebrities parade for the camera. But, not everything is as it seems. Photographs and even films can be altered to make people look better than they really are, and then there's all the money they spend on stylists! Being thin isn't the only way to be beautiful, we are all different and unique, and remember – personality counts towards attractiveness.

eating disorders

When people become obsessed with their body and how they think they look, they can develop an eating disorder. This is when people try to change their body using bad eating habits. Eating disorders are especially dangerous during puberty because your body is growing at a terrific rate and needs nutrition. The eating disorder that most commonly affects adolescents is called anorexia nervosa.

We grow up with unrealistic images of the human body, and this can make us think we aren't shaping-up to the ideal.

IMPOSSIBLE

Eating disorders are normally associated with girls. However, new figures now show one in ten anorexia cases are boys.

anorexia

Anorexia is when someone severely limits his or her eating to lose weight. Here are the danger signs:

* losing loads of weight
* continuing to diet although thin
* feeling fat, even after losing weight
* feeling anxious about gaining weight
* fussy eating
* obsessing about food
* not eating with family or friends

what to do...

If you think you may have anorexia, it is very important to talk to your GP immediately, or to a trusted adult. Even if it is scary to get help, your life may depend on it.

how to help a friend

This can be tricky. Often, people with eating disorders don't want to talk about their problems. Don't let this stop you. People with anorexia often need their friends or family to take the first steps to get help for them. Be patient with your friends and always offer a listening ear. Most importantly, tell a parent or teacher about your worries. Alternatively, you can call the BEAT helpline on 0845 634 1414, which specializes in eating-disorder advice and support for individuals and families.

bulimia

People with this eating disorder go to extreme measures to control their weight. Sufferers secretly eat lots of food. These excessive moments are known as binge-eating. After binge-eating sufferers force themselves to vomit.

SPOTS

Just when you least want one, you feel that tell-tale soren
sense the brewing infection, and there it is – a spot! Pimple
blemishes, acne, whatever you call them, spots are a pa
Everyone hates them, but nearly everyone has to
deal with them at some point.

Why now?

When puberty begins, the oil glands on your
head, face, and elsewhere on your body
become more active. Excess oil can get
trapped by a hair follicle so it can't empty
out of the pores on your skin as it usually
does. Instead the oil builds up and forms a
small plug in the pore, which results in spots.
They can appear on your face, neck,
shoulders, and back.

Facts about acne

- Acne is most common among tee
- 80% of all people between ages
  have acne outbreaks at some pc
- Women develop acne earlier ar
  more likely to have it as adult
- Men are ten times more likely to
  from a severe form of acne.
- 40% of teens have acne that rec
  treatment from a doctor.
- Serious outbreaks can cause emoti
  social problems – low self-confide
  well as poor body image, and feeli
  embarrassment, and frustratio
- No one can help having acn

Normal hair follicle
Tiny open pores on your skin
secrete an oily substance called
sebum. Hormones can cause the
skin to over-produce sebum.

hair
free flow
of sebum
sebum
sebaceous
gland

Blackhead
If the pore becomes blocked,
a blackhead forms like a cap.

dark,
pigmented
plug
sebum
builds up
sebum
sebaceous
gland

Infected follicle
Underneath, the trap
breed bacteria. The a
inflamed and a zit ap

The life and death of an annoying spot

'Mmmm! it feels nice and greasy here!'

A spot starts in a blocked oil gland.

"How to get a-head! Hee, hee, hee!"

Bacteria build-up at the site makes a painful red bump.

'Ugh! I keep getting attacked!'

Cells in your blood rush to fight the infection, producing white pus.

'I'll be back!'

That, combined with a treatment from the chemist, and the spot starts to die.

How to fight back

Different cures work for different people. From over-the-counter spot creams, to natural remedies like tea-tree oil, to antibiotic lotions and pills on prescription from the doctor, it's a case of finding what works for you.

General rules:

- Wash your face with warm water twice a day.
- Don't overdo it with harsh soaps and cleansers.
- Some sunlight on your skin is good for you (but never burn).
- Keep dirty hands off!
- If you must squeeze a spot, wash your hands first and stop once the pus is out. Squeezing out blood or clear fluid damages your skin. Afterwards, dab with a mild antiseptic. Do not squeeze a red spot.
- If you get persistent spots and it's affecting your life, see a doctor.

SPOT MYTHS

Can you *spot* the true statements among these acne myths?

1. Eating chocolate and chips causes spots.
2. Having a dirty face means you get spots.
3. Changing hormone levels 2 to 7 days before a menstrual period can make spots worse.
4. A bit of sun makes spots better.
5. Squeezing, popping, or picking zits will make them go away.
6. Pressure from sports helmets or equipment, backpacks, tight collars, or tight sports uniforms can cause spots.
7. Using heavy, greasy skin-care products can cause spots.

ANSWER: numbers 3, 4, 6, and 7 are true.

Tea tree oil

Spot cream

It's a *jungle*

Playground relationships can sometimes seem like they are straight out of a nature documentary. Read these common playground traits, and **see if you recognize any of them going on in YOUR school playground.**

Here's an experiment that was conducted on teenagers: teenagers took control in a driving simulation.

Players are encouraged to drive as far as they can in a fixed amount of time. Along the way, each player comes across eight traffic lights that turn yellow as the intersection is approached.

Lions It's completely natural for some children to take the lead in playground activities. Every prehistoric tribe (and we are all directly related to the cavemen), like every pack of lions, needed a leader in order to work successfully. Too many people trying to lead the pack weaken it rather than strengthen it.

 Sheep If there are leaders, there have to be followers, and, like sheep, many people don't like to stand out of the crowd. After all, it's always the leader who gets blamed for anything that goes wrong. Through puberty you may find you want to look and behave more like your mates than ever before.

 Monkeys People like to stay in groups for the same reason monkeys go round in troops. It gives us a sense of belonging and provides protection. Even though we don't need to protect ourselves from wild animals anymore, being part of a group still makes us feel safer and happier. As we hit puberty this feeling intensifies.

 Peacocks Just like the peacock showing off its beautiful plumage, some kids have all the gear. Human beings have always used objects to show how powerful or important they are. While our cavemen ancestors may have counted their sheep, today's children like to show off the latest trainers or mp3 player.

 Chameleons Some kids are real chameleons – they change their look, friends, and style, and get on with everyone. These kids are usually friendly and fun. They make great friends, but don't expect to have them to yourself.

The player is faced with a dilemma: stop, and waste time, or go and risk crashing. When adolescents play the game, they take twice as many chances if their peers are in the room than if they are by themselves. No such peer effect is seen among adults.

I wished to be accepted and be part of the group. This is a very important aspect of being human – it's a powerful feeling to an adolescent like me.

BULLYING

We are all different and we start and finish puberty at different times. Unfortunately, these *physical* and *emotional differences* can lead to *bullying*.

WHAT IS BULLYING?

Bullying is when a person, or a group of people, deliberately torment, taunt, and tease you. The abuse can be verbal or physical, making you feel frightened and miserable. Intimidation like this can force you to stay away from places, or friendship groups, that you have every right to be in and enjoy.

WHAT MAKES A BULLY?

There are many reasons why people bully. Most of the time bullies have their own problems and many have been bullied themselves. Also, a lack of understanding about what the body is going through and how to deal with it can lead to bullying. Bullies use differences, whether they are physical, racial, or sexual, to gain the upper hand. Sometimes, these differences can be as petty as being new to a town or school. The smallest thing can give a bully ammunition, and encourage him or her to show off in front of a group.
People who encourage bullies are bullies themselves.

TYPES OF BULLYING

- **PHYSICAL** – From punching and kicking to the physical damage or theft of a victim's belongings.
- **VERBAL** – Name-calling can be deeply hurtful and is common in all aspects of bullying.
- **SEXUAL** – Touching, insinuating, and pressuring the victim to perform or endure acts they don't understand or enjoy.
- **CYBER** – Harassment using new technologies like email, texting, and instant messaging, has become a powerful weapon for bullies to invade a victim's private space, meaning they can bully 24/7 no matter where their victim is.
- **REJECTION** – Ignoring and pushing victims out of friendship groups, clubs, or activities can be used by groups of bullies to victimize and alienate.

HOW TO DEAL WITH IT
Don't suffer in silence... TELL, TELL!

Check out your school's anti-bullying policy and act on what you discover.

Don't feel ashamed. Tell your parents or teacher. They are there to help and support you.

Find it hard to talk to your parents or teachers?
Then phone
Childline 0800 1111

**Bullying is unacceptable, full stop.
If you know it is going on, tell someone in authority.
You can stay anonymous if you want to.**

GROUPS VS GANGS

Friendship is a great relief during puberty. Realizing everyone is in the same boat can build and strengthen relationships. However, it can also be a time of pressure, especially from peers. Make sure your friendships are with the right people.

GROUPS

FRIENDSHIP GROUPS are normally formed around a mutual interest, like sport, movies, music, or just because you all like one another. This similar outlook brings together like-minded people who enjoy each other's company.

Being a member of a group allows you to have fun with friends, as well as create your own individual identity.

GOOD FRIENDS
are...
Loyal
Trustworthy
Honest
Supportive
Good listeners

REMEMBER Childhood is about having FUN and ENJOYING yourself. If you

GANGS

GANGS on the other hand aren't quite what they seem. They share similar traits to friendship groups, though instead of being an individual, GANGS promote a mimic mentality and you can be forced to put the GANG's reputation before your own or your friends'. This can lead to trouble, especially during puberty when understanding and finding yourself is so important.

BAD FRIENDS
are...
Sneaky
Manipulative
Selfish
Pressurising
Put you down

I JUST FELT LIKE IT!

If the only reason you can think of for doing a particularly risky antic is that you did it because you **just felt like it**, then you may be able to **blame** it on your **brain**. After all, you could say, your **basal ganglia**, the part of your brain that helps your **frontal cortex** (in charge of logical thinking) is not fully developed yet!

SCIENTISTS noticed some differences between the sexes. Girls' and boys' brains develop at different rates.

Amygdala grows faster in teen boys – this is responsible for gut reaction and **emotion**.

Cerebellum is 14% larger in boys – this is important for **physical coordination**.

The hippocampus, crucial for many **memory tasks**, grows faster in girls.

BASAL GANGLIA

AMYGDALA

CEREBELLUM

HIPPOCAMPUS

Spurs in brain development, not sudden bouts of madness, they say, may help explain why kids start caring about different things, acting in new ways, and taking risks as they make the transition to adulthood.

The adolescent brain is a work in progress. Scientists have found out that even though the size of the brain changes by only five percent at this time, the size of its different parts does change a lot.

LEAVE

KEEP OUT

As you reach puberty, you may find your parents start *bugging you* — even more than usual! *What's going on?* You are turning into an **adult**, and leaving your role of child behind.

This can put strain on the child/parent relationship, as you naturally want to stretch the bonds. It is all a necessary part of growing up, and most parents understand this and give new privileges. However, sometimes conflict can result.

COMMON CAUSES OF FIGHTS WITH YOUR FOLKS!

You want to go to the festival in the park. All your friends are going. Your parents say NO!

**!*?!?*
They make you go on family trips with them, when you'd prefer to be with your friends.

You want your ears pierced/hair dyed. Your parents object.

Your parents limit your computer use or won't let you watch certain TV shows.

Your parents don't like a new set of friends you've made.

In fact, this list could go on for quite a long time, and sometimes life at home can feel a bit like a tug of war, especially as you hit the teen years.

ME ALONE!

Take these points into consideration

- Your parents love you and want the best for you. They are not trying to ruin your life!
- Parents worry about their children, sometimes too much, but it comes from the heart.
- Parents need to adapt to you turning into an adult too. They may find it hard to let go of their baby.
- Parents have house rules, and, just because you are growing up, it doesn't mean they go out of the window.

What can we do about it?

- COMPROMISE and BARGAINING – it's always worth a try!
- Being TRUSTWORTHY is a major winner with the folks. If you can prove you are this time and again, you will be allowed to do more.
- Always let them know WHERE you are, WHO you're with, what TIME you'll be back, and keep to it. You don't have to tell them every detail but doing this will stop them worrying.

DO NOT ENTER

WORLDS APART?

I like your shoes, where did you get them?

From Shooz in the mall. They have them in blue and red too! By the way, while I was in the shops I saw Trudie. Remember her? She said she was still friends with Rosie Lloyd!

Girls' talk?

Girls tend to talk about other people. They tell each other secrets, discuss school, and talk about things they want and need. They may also like talking about boys and clothes. Girls communicate using words, and are good at talking about feelings.

Girls think boys...

... are immature (try having a serious talk with one!).

... show off and use bad language to try to act cool.

... think they are super-strong (all brawn, no brain!).

... take the mick and goof around.

But boys can also be...

... courteous, helpful, thoughtful, and kind.

Try not to judge the opposite sex, or clump them together.

Men and women often find it hard to understand each other. In fact some say it's as though they come from different planets. But are **BOYS** really show-offs? And are *girls* bitchy? It's easy to generalize, but much better to look at people as individuals.

Check out my mp3 player. It's the new classic with 160 gig storage. That's like 40,000 songs. And it plays video!

Cool. Did you see the match on Sunday? I went with my dad, it was wicked. Richard Coggins scored a hat trick! He can't stop scoring, that's like 30 for the season. He reminds me a bit of myself when I play!

BOYS'
talk?

Boys talk about things and activities — sports, mechanics, and how and why things work. Boys express their emotions through actions rather than words. They may hit out if they're angry, or withdraw to be silent and alone if they're hurt or upset.

Boys think girls…
… are bitchy, always ganging up on each other, with lashing tongues.
… are shopaholics and always talking about shops, sales, clothes, accessories, shoes, and jewellery…
… are scaredy cats — scared of the dark, storms, spiders…
… are capricious — always changing their minds.
… and never stop talking — about nothing much!

But girls can also be…
… loyal, reserved, honest, and brave.

Everyone is an individual with a mixture of qualities.

100% BOY

What makes

BOYS

boys?

BOYS and GIRLS are different – it's a fact of life. So, what's going on under your skin that makes you a boy? Boys and girls are almost exactly the same, but with four important differences...

① hormones

Testosterone! This powerful sex hormone makes boys, boys. It has always been flowing around your body. But between the ages of 11 and 14 there is a huge rise in testosterone levels. This increase helps kick-start puberty and affects how you think, grow, and behave.

penis | testicle

② sex organs

The male sex organs hang outside the body. They are the penis and the two testicles (the testes). When hormones trigger puberty, the testes begin to produce sperm and extra testosterone.

Every day a man makes between 50 and 500 million sperm in his testes, and the sperm take 1–3 weeks to mature.

③ the brain

Scientists have long been interested in testing for differences between the brains of boys and girls.

There are several physical differences between boys' and girls' brains. Boys' brains are bigger than girls' brains – unfortunately that doesn't make us more intelligent. Also, boys' brains mature more slowly than girls', but we do catch up eventually. A boy's brain is also good at judging distance and size, as well as making mental maps.

④ chromosomes

The sex chromosomes are one of the 23 pairs you have inside every body cell. Sex chromosomes are shaped like the letters X or Y. They determine whether you are a boy or a girl. You inherit one chromosome from each parent. If you have an X and a Y, then you're a boy. If you have two Xs, then you would be a girl.

X chromosome   Y chromosome

Your chromosomes are made of DNA and carry genetic (inherited) instructions that make you, you. You have a pair of XY chromosomes in every body cell. That means every single body cell "knows" you're a boy. Man, that's a lot of knowing cells – over 10 trillion!

Boys' bodies

Our bodies change all the time – that's part and parcel of growing up and getting old. Men have three main phases in their life cycle.

1 Childhood

This fun-filled phase starts at birth and ends when puberty and adolescence begins.

2 Puberty

The transition phase from childhood into adulthood. Your body and feelings change dramatically as you become capable of fathering a child.

Body types

During puberty your body changes shape and size. How it changes is all down to your genes, the amount of tissue types, and the levels of chemicals, like hormones, in your body.

REMEMBER These body types are general categories. See them as extreme points on a triangle, depending on your genes you may be a mixture of the three.

ENDO MAN

ENDOMORPHIC (Apple body)

This body type has a wider waist and a large bone structure. An increase in fat-cell production gives a fuller figure, especially on the top half of the body.

3 Adulthood

You are now fully grown and have responsibilities, though don't forget to have fun!

A GROWING CONCERN

One thing men have to endure, which most women don't, is baldness. Like so much stuff with your body, this is connected to your genes. It can start at any age, including your teenage years. It's hard to cope with, but remember there is little you can do about it and it only affects how you look – it's not an illness or a disability.

Unlike the female body, the male body **DOESN'T** go through a menopause **stage.** But, fertility does DECREASE as the body ages, though men can be fertile well into old age.

Keep going men, nearly there.....

Les Colley of Australia was **92** when he fathered his *ninth* child!

100% boy

MESO MAN

MESOMORPHIC (Rectangle body)

This is the more beefy body type with more muscle growth. Larger bones and low fat levels combine with wide shoulders to give a stocky appearance.

ECTO MAN

ECTOMORPHIC (Banana body)

This is the slim body type. Arms and legs are long with a short upper body and narrow shoulders.

TESTOSTERONE

Testosterone is the main male **sex hormone** that helps kick-start puberty. It is produced in the testes and triggers sperm production, as well as prompting your **body to grow** and change. Testosterone doesn't just affect how you look on the outside – it also alters your *emotions* and how you feel on the inside.

Increased aggression

The huge surge in testosterone levels (800% more than when you were a toddler) during puberty can have some side effects. While it helps make you fit and strong, and can even help your emotional well-being, it can also make you more quick to anger and aggressive. It also triggers body hair and muscle growth, as well as making your voice break.

I think therefore I am... moody!

Hormonal upheaval can trigger emotional upheaval. You may become more self-conscious and experience **mood swings**. Many boys cry a lot more during early puberty. Don't worry. It's *perfectly normal*.

Feeling sexy?

As testosterone levels rise you will also begin to **produce more sperm** in your testes. This makes you have more **sexual feelings.** These feelings are new and they may take some getting used to. It's worth bearing in mind that although testosterone can make you feel different in lots of different ways, you don't have to act on any new feelings you may have.

BOY >> MAN

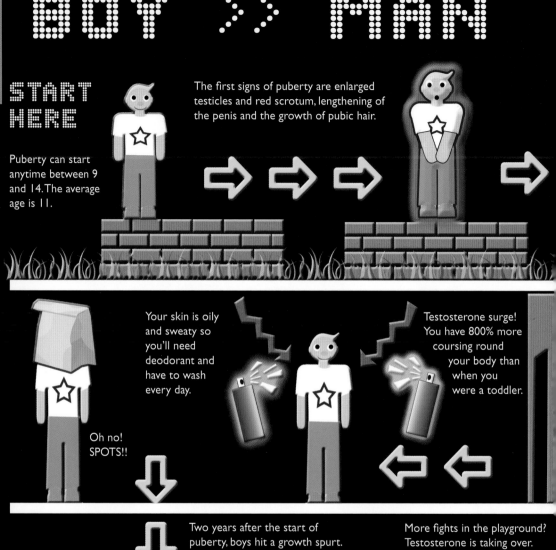

START HERE

Puberty can start anytime between 9 and 14. The average age is 11.

The first signs of puberty are enlarged testicles and red scrotum, lengthening of the penis and the growth of pubic hair.

Your skin is oily and sweaty so you'll need deodorant and have to wash every day.

Oh no! SPOTS!!

Testosterone surge! You have 800% more coursing round your body than when you were a toddler.

Two years after the start of puberty, boys hit a growth spurt. (Though, not all boys are tall...)

More fights in the playground? Testosterone is taking over.

Some boys get really muscly,. Don't worry if you don't – everyone's different.

Body hair – everywhere!

By mid-teens, you may need to start shaving.

Puberty can be a *challenge*, so it's good to know what to expect, when. Follow the *arrows* to learn the *stages*. (Keep in mind that this is a general guide. Everybody is different.)

Hmmm... Hairy armpits!

The voice box enlarges and your vocal cords grow. A high voice starts to deepen.

Watch out for those mid-sentence, high-pitched "SQUEAKS"!

...nd ...oluntary ...ections.

Damp pyjamas and sheets?

First involuntary ejaculation...

Wet dreams start to happen

Now you can enjoy some of the good things about getting older!

WELL DONE... *you made it!*

Vrrroom!

...ong sexual urges... normal.

Outside and in

The *male sex organs* are mainly on the outside of the body. Because of this their *change* and *growth* is very noticeable. Let's take a quick look *outside* and *in* at what they are all about and what to expect during puberty.

on the outside...

Male sex organs all look different. Here's a general look at what's hanging where and why.

PENIS HEAD/TIP (Glans penis)
This is the most sensitive part of the penis. It's this area, once stimulated, that leads to ejaculation. There is an opening on the penis tip, called the meatus, where urine and semen exit the body.

SCROTUM
This pouch of skin hangs below the penis and contains and protects the testes.

FORESKIN
This sensitive layer of skin covers and protects the tip of the penis.

FRENULUM
This is the thin piece of tissue that connects the foreskin to the penis tip.

WHAT HAPPENED TO MY FORESKIN?

Not everyone has a foreskin. This is because at birth, or even as adults, you can have it removed. This is called circumcision and is usually for religious beliefs or medical reasons. Even though the penis looks different, it acts in the same way.

foreskin

penis tip

Uncircumcised penis

Circumcised penis

STAGES OF GROWTH

The appearance of your sex organs changes a lot during puberty.

1 PRE-PUBERTY
The penis grows with the rest of your body. It's small and only has one purpose – peeing.

2 EARLY YEARS OF PUBERTY
The testes start to grow. The scrotum skin thins and becomes darker and wrinkly.

3 MID-PUBERTY
The penis will start to lengthen. Pubic hair begins to grow.

4 LATE PUBERTY
The penis becomes wider and the tip more prominent. Pubic hair darkens, thickens and becomes curly.

5 POST PUBERTY
Growth is complete.

on the inside...

It's easy to see and feel what's happening on the outside. But what's going on under the skin – how's it all connected? Here's an insight into the inside...

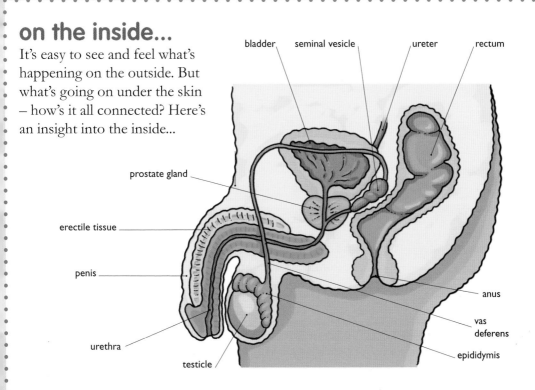

bladder   seminal vesicle   ureter   rectum

prostate gland

erectile tissue

penis

urethra

testicle

anus

vas deferens

epididymis

TESTES (testicles)
These are men's sexual factories. They produce the male sex cells (sperm), as well as the sex hormone testosterone.

URETHRA
This tube connects the bladder to the tip of the penis. It allows urine to exit the body. It is also used as a passageway for semen. When this happens access from the bladder is cut off, allowing the semen to travel up and out of the penis.

EPIDIDYMIS AND THE VAS DEFERENS
Both testicles are capped by an epididymis. This is a small tube-like structure where sperm mature and get ready for their journey. Each vas deferens is a flexible tube up to 30 cm (12 in) long, that connects the epididymis to the urethra.

PROSTATE GLAND AND THE SEMINAL VESICLES
These glands produce the milky fluid that mixes with the sperm to create semen. Being suspended in the fluid allows the sperm to flow easily along their journey.

SEMEN
Approximately 70% of semen is fluid from the seminal vesicles, and 25% is fluid from the prostate. Only 5% of semen is sperm.

erectile tissue

ERECTION
How does the penis get hard? **ERECTILE TISSUES** run the length of the penis. When the penis is stimulated the tissues fill with blood, making them grow and harden. When erect, the penis curves upwards slightly towards the belly.

erect penis

Living with "John Thomas"

Having a penis isn't always smooth sailing. There are many hidden quirks and annoyances waiting to happen, especially during puberty. Here's a run down on what to expect living with your penis.

Standing to attention

One thing that becomes more prominent during puberty is the erection. What's its purpose? It's all linked to reproduction. But you guys are all too young for that, so let's have a look at why it's happening now and why you can't always control it.

What is happening

An erection is a bit like blowing up a balloon. Instead of air, it's blood filling erectile tissues making the soft penis harden and grow.

When and why?

To start with erections can be hard to control – it happens to everyone. Here are a few examples of when your penis can stand to attention:

• when you are nervous or excited.
• when you need to pee.
• while sleeping.
• and for no reason whatsoever!

Coping with erections

One of the more embarrassing erections you will face is the spontaneous kind. They happen for no reason, it's just your body getting used to the new sex hormones. Here are a few handy hints to help you deal with them:

• baggy clothes can conceal them.
• sit down to hide it.
• shield it with a bag or book.
• think about something else until it goes away.

Sperm factory

Your body will start to produce sperm at a terrific rate, on average 1,500 sperm every second, per testicle – that's nearly 260 million every day! This persistent build-up leaves the living space in your testes very cramped, so your body needs to release the excess sperm. This is achieved by ejaculation.

Wet dreams and masturbation

Boys will usually experience their first ejaculation between the ages of 11–15. Ejaculation is the release of semen, which contains sperm. A **wet dream** is when ejaculation occurs involuntarily during sleep. **Masturbation** is a self-triggered ejaculation. As you stroke your penis you will feel a pleasureable sensation that builds into an orgasm. This is normally accompanied by ejaculation.

SIZING-UP

The first place to start with size is not to. There are only average statistics out there and averages never paint the true picture. Basically, you are the size you are supposed to be. At the end of it all, the penis's main role is for reproduction, and the vagina fits around it whatever shape or size.

What's a tallywacker?

The male genitals have always been an awkward conversational subject and some people find it hard to say penis. So, here are a few alternatives you may hear it called.

HELLO
my name is
JOHN THOMAS

penis (general)
John Thomas
knob
manhood
tallywacker
sausage
member
prick
dick
trouser snake
Johnson
willy
winkle
dinkle

erect penis
woody
boner
hard-on
stiffy

testicles
balls
ball bag
goolies
cobblers

**penis
and tesicles**
tackle
meat and two veg
package
lunch box
family jewels
Frank 'n' beans

BODY HAIR
EVERYWHERE

The prospect of growing so much hair can be scary. But **don't worry,** you won't turn into a hairy monster every full moon! Your body **hair will sprout gradually**. Here's a general guide to when and where to expect your hairy transformation.

From boy to man
When it comes to hairiness it's all in your genes. You often take after your parents. So, check out dad to see how hairy you might be.

Body hair – why it's there

Body hair is there for a reason. It traps dirt and germs and helps to keep you clean. Body hair also keeps you warm and protects sensitive areas, like your underarms and genitals.

facial hair usually starts from 14–18 years old, though can start earlier or later. The thickness, coverage, and colour depends on your genes and can change throughout your life. Some men grow full beards, others just moustaches or sideburns.

Fact
An average adult male has about 5,000,000 hair follicles all over his body.

chest hair usually comes towards the end of puberty. Not all men can grow chest hair, though you usually get a little growth around the nipples, even if you are bare-chested.

underarm hair develops between the ages of 11 and 13. This is a good sign you should start washing under your arms every day and look into using deodorant.

arm and leg hair will start to grow darker and coarser. On your legs this will usually start from the pubic region down on to your thighs. Your shins and forearms will also show signs of thicker and darker hair growth.

pubic hair is the first area where hair growth usually starts. At around 11–13 years old, light and soft hairs will start to grow around the base of your penis. These pubic hairs will grow thicker, coarser, and curlier over time.

in the BATHROOM

CLEAN MACHINE

When you're exercising you sweat more, and even emotions like feeling nervous before a test can make your hands and neck feel clammy. You have millions of sweat glands all over your body. During puberty they become more active. More sweat means BODY ODOUR! It's not the sweat that smells but the bacteria that breaks it down. So how do you stop the stink?

DAILY DOSE

The best way to beat B.O. is to wash every day. Bathing and showering with a good gel or soap will wash away the bacteria and keep you fresh and clean. Your genitals and underarms are important areas to target.

ANTI-PERSPIRANT

Another way to avoid B.O. is to reduce the amount you sweat in the first place. Anti-perspirant in a spray or roll-on keeps you drier.

DEODORANTS

Deodorants and body sprays work differently. They only mask the smell. These are better for people who don't sweat as much and can be a good place to start when puberty begins.

STEP UP

Much-forgotten smell villains are your feet. Sweaty feet are a perfect breeding ground for bacteria. Always remember to wash your feet after long walks and exercise.

SWEAT

Odour-eaters for your shoes may be helpful to mask any brewing smells.

You can also get SPECIAL FOOT deodorants to keep your feet dry.

ALSO, WEAR SOCKS!

THEY ABSORB THE SMELL, SO YOUR SHOES WON'T STINK. JUST REMEMBER TO CHANGE YOUR SOCKS EVERY DAY.

There is going to be far *more to do in the bathroom*, shaving, washing, and dealing with spots. Here are a few guidelines to cope with your changing body and keep you smelling and looking good.

A CLOSE SHAVE

Shaving for the first time can be scary – it is also exciting. Here are a few hints and tips to help you master the art of shaving. First there's a choice to be made: ELECTRIC or WET?

ELECTRIC

This is a good starting-out option. It is also quicker and there is less chance of cuts and nicks. However, it doesn't give as close a shave. The best tip is not to force the shaver into your skin, as this can cause irritation.

Never lend or borrow a shaver – you can pass on or get infections!

WET SHAVE

For this you'll need a razor, either a disposable or one with a replaceable blade. Make sure the blade is sharp and clean. Shaving foam and gel allows the razor to glide across the skin and limits soreness. Warm water will soften your hairs and make them easier to cut.

SMILE!

Puberty can also cause bad breath, which can affect your social life. A healthy smile lasts for life, so it's best to lay the groundwork now with a regular and thorough cleaning routine. It can seem boring, but it makes visits to the DENTIST'S CHAIR a lot easier.

MAKE SURE YOU BRUSH YOUR TEETH AT LEAST TWICE A DAY. DON'T FORGET YOUR GUMS AND TONGUE, WHERE BACTERIA CAN BREED.

RINSE

A mouth wash can fight decay and also helps mask any foul smells.

Another helpful hint that battles bad breath is drinking water after eating. It helps wash away bacteria and food, and keeps your mouth fresh.

BAD BREATH

WHAT CAUSES IT? IT'S THOSE PESKY BACTERIA AGAIN. THEY BREAK DOWN THE BITS OF FOOD THAT GET TRAPPED IN YOUR TEETH.

FLOSSING

removes the stubborn food bits.

Man TALK

One of the most obvious and embarrassing things about puberty is when your voice breaks. Reading aloud or even talking to friends can be a minefield of high-pitched squeaks, but why?

YOUR VOICE BOX

Your voice comes from a box-shaped hollow in your throat that contains your vocal cords. Air vibrates up through the box to create sounds. During puberty, testosterone makes your voice box grow up to 60% bigger. This changes how you sound.

GULP!

YOUR VOCAL CORDS

Inside the voice box are your vocal cords. These increase in size and thickness and make your voice get deeper. Think of them like the strings on a guitar. When you pluck the thinner string it vibrates at a higher pitch – a bit like your childhood vocal cords. The thicker string vibrates at a lower pitch – like your new deeper adult vocal cords.

VOICE BOX

Adam's apple

vocal cords

eek!

EMBARRASSING SQUEAKS

Voice breaking can throw up some annoying sound bites. When your vocal cords grow you will struggle to control your voice and it can break out in random high-pitched squeaks. Remember, like playing a new instrument, you're not going to sound perfect straight away. And yes, it can be embarrassing, but try to laugh with it, there's nothing you can do about it and once your voice box has finished growing you won't get them anymore.

GROWING APPLES

When your voice box grows, it can stick out from your neck. This bump is known as your Adam's apple. For some boys it is more noticeable than others. Its size is down to how big your voice box grows.

squeak!

GIRL TALK

Girls' voices also change during puberty. It might not sound that way, but they get deeper and girls grow an Adam's apple too. However, they have less testosterone, so the change isn't as noticeable.

Growing pains

A group of 13-year-old boys can all look very different. Some are tall with facial hair and muscles, some are in-between, and some are still boys. Whether you develop early or late, growing up can be a pain.

THE BIG AND SMALL OF IT

The sports field is an arena where differences in size and strength can throw up particular challenges. During puberty, team sports can pit smaller boys against taller, stronger boys. If you are one of the smaller boys, this can make you stop enjoying sports that you previously loved.

So, what can you do to level the playing field?

IF YOU ARE
SMALLER...

1. Concentrate on **dexterity,** *balance,* and FITNESS – these will be vital as your body becomes stronger.

2. Take up a SENSIBLE training regime to help strengthen and build your muscles.

3. Look beyond the sports field – maybe you have other *talents* like music, writing, or drawing.

GROWING PAINS

You might feel aches and pains in your limbs without getting injured, these are known as GROWING PAINS and are common during puberty as you grow quickly. They will fade with time, but if persistent, again, always see your family GP.

Don't let size put you off. You will grow and get bigger and better. Be patie

IF YOU ARE BIGGER...

1. You could act as a **LEADER** in your team and encourage the smaller players.

2. If team sports aren't to your taste then try *individual sports* like boxing or athletics.

3. It might be possible to change your role in the team, while others catch up – this also allows you to learn new skills.

GYNECOMASTIA

Men don't grow breasts like women, but during puberty the surge and imbalance of hormones rushing through your body means you may experience a degree of gynecomastia – growing breast tissue. Don't worry if you do – up to 65% of boys suffer from a degree of it.

What to look out for...

The chest area will grow breast tissue, this can be quite prominent or hardly noticeable under the nipple. The region can become tender and itchy.

Gynecomastia can be disturbing, but it is only temporary and it will go down in a couple of months to a year. If it persists or becomes uncomfortable, it is always best to see your family GP.

...and don't give up – you might even hit a growth spurt and tower over everyone.

Keeping FIT

Exercise and sport are a great way to keep fit and healthy. This is important during puberty because your muscles have to deal with your bigger and heavier body. The effort you put in now will keep you strong and healthy as adulthood approaches.

Try a new sport

With boys growing at different rates, sports that you once enjoyed might start to feel physically unfair and less fun. It is always worth persevering, but you could also try something new. How about a martial art, or golf? Or you could try your hand at hockey. There's a sport out there for everyone, whatever shape and size you are.

Hockey

Golf

Karate

Warm up

When you were a child you were naturally stretchy and flexible, unlike your parents. As your body grows during puberty your muscles have more work to do and will tire more quickly. To keep you going on the sports field and reduce injuries you have to warm up and stretch.

Stretching

Stretching increases the strength and flexibility of your muscles, making you jump, run, and reach further. It's important to stretch your back and shoulders, arms and waist, as well as your trunk (torso muscles). And don't forget your legs. Here are four stretches to start you off.

Thigh stretch

Standing on one leg, balance yourself and grab your foot. Gently pull your leg up towards your bum. Hold for 10–20 seconds on each leg.

Hamstring stretch

Keeping your weight on your heels, place one leg in front of the other. Keep your knees relaxed and gently bend. Hold for 10–20 seconds on each leg.

Groin stretch

Sit with your heels together. With your elbows on your knees, slowly allow your knees to drop towards the floor. Hold for 10–20 seconds.

Calf stretch

Stand with one leg in front of the other. Slowly and gently bend your front knee while keeping your back heel on the ground. Hold for 10–20 seconds.

Changing rooms

Changing in front of other boys for P.E. and sports can be worrying. Puberty happens at different times for everyone and inevitably boys will compare each other. If you are worried, you can always change facing the wall. If you are teased and it's distressing, you should tell your teacher.

CRUSHES & LOVE

When puberty steps up a gear, the way you see and feel about girls will change. Your body will start to produce more sex hormones, which trigger new sexual feelings. With all these new feelings, you'll need to know how to handle crushes and deal with rejection.

CRUSHES

A CRUSH IS WHEN YOU HAVE ROMANTIC FEELINGS ABOUT SOMEONE. JUST SEEING THEM CAN MAKE YOUR DAY. SOMETIMES YOU MIGHT DEVELOP A CRUSH ON SOMEONE WHO ISN'T ATTAINABLE, SUCH AS AN OLDER GIRL, YOUR TEACHER, OR EVEN A POP STAR. THESE CAN BE HEALTHY, ALLOWING YOU TO IMAGINE AND PLAY WITH YOUR NEW FEELINGS, BUT WATCH OUT FOR THE DANGER OF CRUSHES.

DANGER of crushes

If you step too far and think it is possible to have a romance with someone who isn't interested or attainable you can set yourself up for being hurt. When you are young and have strong, new feelings it is easy to think they are love. Watch out, crushes can make you obsess about people – you think about them and try to see them all the time. This can be anti-social and put people off you. Always try to keep your crush in perspective. When someone doesn't like you back, it is hard to deal with this rejection, even when you are older and more mature.

Sexuality

Most adults are considered to be heterosexual. This is when you prefer to have sexual relationships with someone of the opposite sex. However, this isn't the only path open to you. You might find yourself having strong feelings toward someone of the same sex. This can be a feeling of admiration or romance. Many people have a homosexual experience, feeling, or dream. This is perfectly normal and does not necessarily mean you are homosexual. You are only considered to be homosexual or gay if, as an adult, you prefer sexual relationships with men. You might also hear the term bisexuality. This is when an adult has an equal sexual attraction to both men and women. No matter what you are, it is a healthy, normal part of you, and nothing to be ashamed of.

REJECTION

The people you are attracted to will not always like you back, and vice-versa. This can happen both in friendships and crushes. Rejection is hard to take and it will hurt. The only thing that can help is knowing it happens to everyone and after time it will fade and you will move on.

DOES she like me?

Butterflies in your stomach? Nervous about saying the wrong thing? Liking a girl isn't easy. And the fact you have to make the first move doesn't make it any easier. But, how can you work out if someone likes you too? Here's a quiz to help you read those signs.

1. How long have you known her?

A Days / Weeks

B Months

C Years

2. How do her friends act around you?

A They don't, they just ignore me.

B Friendly, but don't talk about her.

C They tease me about her.

3. How does she act with you when you're with your friends?

A She ignores me.

B She treats me like everyone else in the group.

C She playfully teases me.

4. How does she act with you when you are alone?

A We are never alone.

B We get on well.

C She seems nervous and shy.

5. When you do talk, what are the conversations like?

A She seems uninterested.

B She only talks about my friend.

C She is interested in what I say.

6. When you pass in the corridor at school does she…

A … not realize you exist.

B … wave, but keep on talking to her friends.

C … match your stare and smiles.

FIRST STEPS

It's all well and good thinking someone likes you, but what's to stop you being wrong and making a fool of yourself? You have to find out for sure, and to do this you are going to have to talk to her. This might seem daunting, but one way of seeing if a girl likes you is to ask.

You can do this in two ways.
1. Scary as it seems, you could speak to her and find out.
2. A little less daunting is to ask a trustworthy friend to ask her for you, or at least to ask her friends.

RIGHT TIME RIGHT PLACE

The time and place are also key when finding out, or telling a girl you like her. You don't want to get off on the wrong foot and embarrass her in front of the class. Try a more private place, like at the park or a friend's party.

Just friends
Mostly
Bs

Not interested

Mostly
As

Maybe love

Mostly
Cs

IT'S UP TO YOU

Once you know she likes you too, then what? Well, one thing is for certain, and that's be yourself. Don't try to change just to gain affection – it won't work out in the long run. Just be friendly and confident and have fun!

AWKWARD SILENCES

Silences can be awkward, but don't panic and try to fill them with the first thing that comes into your head – you might say something you don't mean. Relax and think of something she might want to talk about. Teasing each other is fun, but remember not to take it too far. Laughing together is cool, laughing at someone isn't.

Puberty can seem like it's all about *perspiration* and **PIMPLES**

"*It's* PANTS!

Mood swings. Your fuse is short and you argue more with your parents and friends.

Voice breaking! Watch out for those high-pitched squeaks.

Spots! Just when you start to hope that girls will find you attractive, these pop up all over your face!

Hairy you. Hairs sprout all over your body and you have to face up to the tricky art of shaving.

Your body is changing and you have no control. You'll need to wash and deodorize every day to stop the stink.

Wet dreams. Embarrassing mornings deciding whether you should own up or hide your sheets.

Spontaneous erections. He pops up when you least want or expect it.

...ere are some reasons why it's *pants*, and some reasons why it's not all *that* BAD.

It's GREAT! ""

You grow taller and stronger into a man-sized version of you.

Masturbation is an enjoyable new hobby.

Adulthood – many of life's journeys and adventures begin! One step closer to finishing school! And you get to stay out later.

You gain independence, but remember it comes with responsibility, like organizing your own money.

And at the end of it all you can go to uni and vote and get your voice heard. Puberty is gradual, it doesn't happen overnight. So, there's plenty of time to get used to it and have fun.

Only a few years until you can learn to drive – no more parent taxis.

✓ TRUE OR

1 Boys may start puberty anytime between the ages of 9 and 14.

2 The male sex organs are hidden inside the body.

3 Boys' voices break easily with total control and no squeaks.

4 Boys can sometimes have erections for no reason whatsoever.

5 Wet dreams are normal and you don't have any control over them.

6 It isn't necessary to wash every day – you won't stink because of puberty.

7 Boys and girls can grow an Adam's apple.

FALSE? ✕

8 Adults know nothing about puberty and growing up.

9 Boys all grow at the same time and at the same rate.

10 Masturbating too much will give you hairy palms and reduce your fertility.

11 The tip of the penis is the most sensitive part.

12 Testosterone makes you grow body hair, bigger muscles, and gives you a deeper voice.

13 …but, testosterone has no affect on your mood.

GRRRʀʀ

14 Boys turn into werewolves overnight.

answers: 1. true 2. false 3. false 4. true 5. true 6. false
7. true 8. false 9. false 10. false 11. true 12. true 13. false 14. false

91

Puberty A-Z

Puberty? What does it all mean? It's hard enough to understand what is happening to your body without all these new, long words. Well, here are a few important words and their meanings.

acne inflammation of the skin that causes pimples.

anorexia an eating disorder in which people limit their intake of food to an unhealthy degree.

bisexual being attracted to both men and women.

breasts the two milk-producing organs on the front of a woman's chest.

bulimia an eating disorder in which people eat large amounts of food, then make themselves vomit.

carbohydrates starchy foods, such as bread, rice, and potatoes, that provide energy.

cervix the narrow opening of a woman's uterus.

chromosomes sets of microscopic structures that carry genes inside human cells.

circumcision the removal of the man's foreskin for religious or medical reasons.

clitoris part of the woman's sex organs, this sensitive button-like mound of skin induces sexual pleasure and feelings.

DNA minute threads that carry genes and make up chromosomes.

ejaculation the discharge of semen from the penis during orgasm.

erection the process by which blood flows into the penis, making it firm enough to enter the vagina.

fallopian tubes the channels that carry eggs from a woman's ovaries to her uterus.

fertilization the joining of a sperm cell and an egg cell to create new life.

follicle the tiny hole that surrounds the root of a hair.

genes chemically coded instructions carried by DNA. Genes are passed from parents to children on chromosomes.

heterosexual being attracted to people of the opposite sex.

homosexual being attracted to people of the same sex as you are.

hormones chemical messengers produced by various glands in the body.

masturbation stimulation of the genitals without sexual intercourse. The word usually refers to stimulating yourself by stroking or rubbing.

menstruation monthly discharge of blood and other fluids from the uterus. This happens only when there is no baby growing.

obesity excessively overweight.

oestrogen female sex hormone, made in the ovaries.

orgasm the extreme sensation of pleasure that usually results from sexual stimulation. It takes the form of a series of increasingly strong spasms that build up to a powerful release. Both men and women have orgasms, but only the male orgasm is necessary for reproduction, since it involves the release of semen.

ovaries the two organs in a woman's abdomen that produce eggs and sex hormones.

peer someone in the same social, educational, and age group as you are.

penis the male sexual organ, used to transfer semen to the female during sexual intercourse (and also to carry urine out of the body).

period menstrual period, see menstruation.

pituitary gland small organ attached to the brain that secretes sex and growth hormones.

progesterone female sex hormone, made in the ovaries.

puberty the time when a child's body turns into an adult's body and can therefore reproduce.

pubic hair coarse, curly hair that first grows around the genitals at puberty.

sebum oil secreted by the skin.

sexual intercourse the activity during which the male's erect penis is inserted into the female's vagina, and ejaculation usually takes place.

semen the fluid in which sperm are carried.

sperm male sex cells, produced in the testicles.

testes see testicles.

testicles the two male sexual organs, where sperm are produced and stored.

testosterone male sex hormone, produced in the testicles.

uterus the hollow muscly organ in a woman's body that holds and protects a baby before it's born.

urethra the tube that carries urine out of the body in both men and women. Men's urethras also carry sperm.

vagina the passage that leads from a woman's uterus to the outside of her body. A man's sperm enters, and babies are born, through the vagina.

wet dream the act of ejaculating during sleep.

womb see uterus

Index

we would like to thank...

Leah Germann, Lorrie Mack, Penny Smith, Karen Hood, Carrie Love, Beth Hester, Nancy Ellwood, Michelle Hainer, and Juliet Butler for her illustrations.